GOLD-N-BROWN RULEBOOK

WRITTEN BY JIMMY DAVIS
ILLUSTRATED BY TRENT GERSBACH

PORLIO
PUBLISHING

Copyright © 2021 Jimmy Davis
All rights reserved.

No part of this publication may be reproduced or distributed, in whole or in part, by any means without the prior written permission of the author, except in the case of brief quotations embodied in critical reviews and other noncommercial uses permitted by copyright law.

ISBN: 979-8-9853298-0-3 (Paperback)
ISBN: 979-8-9853298-1-0 (e-book)

Davis, Jimmy, author/creator.
Gersbach, Trent, illustrator/cover-design.
Kip and Clive Present The Gold-n-Brown Rulebook / Jimmy Davis

Printed in the United States

Porlio Publishing

KipandClive.com

Dedicated to our moms who patiently taught us how.
And why.

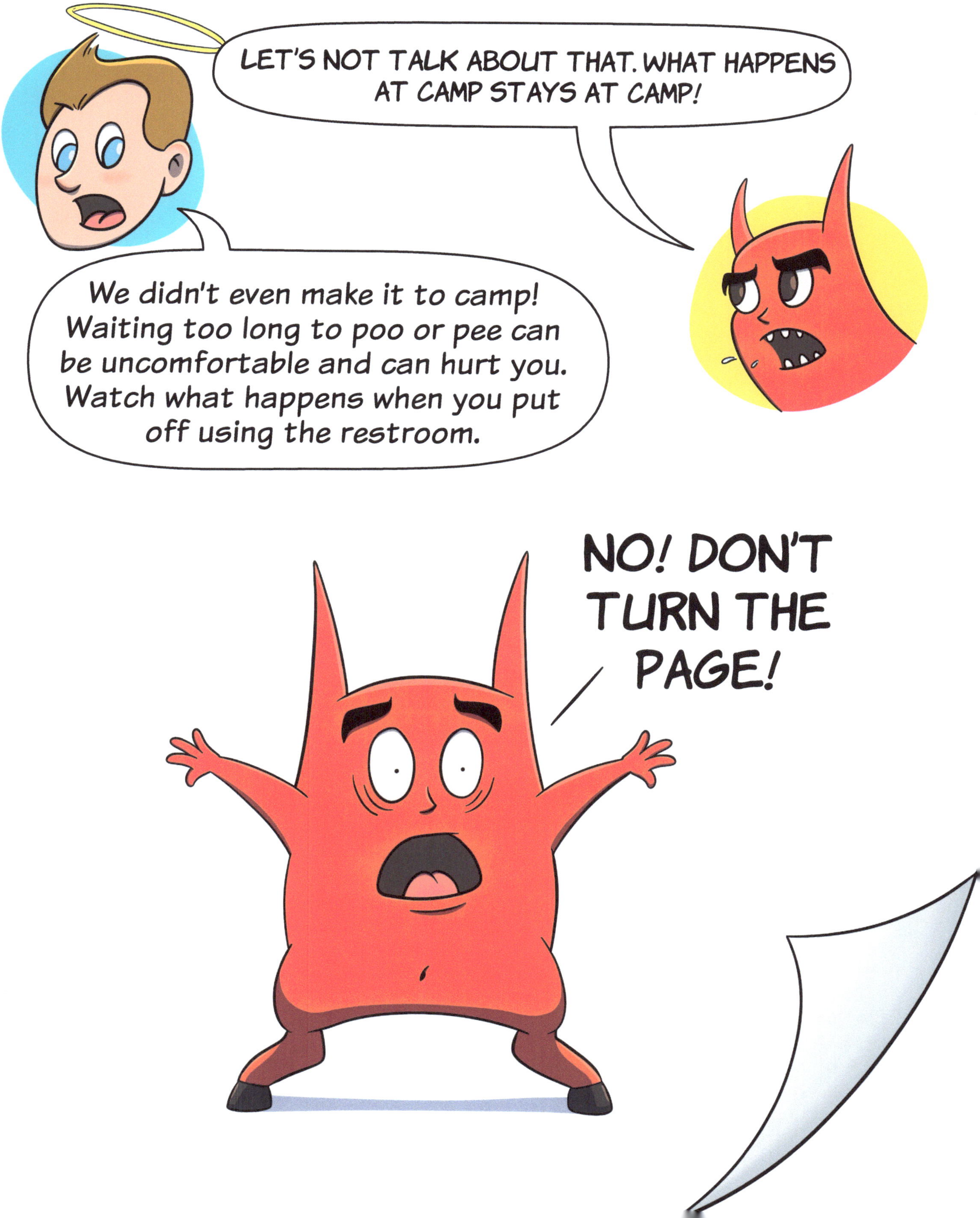

"LET'S NOT TALK ABOUT THAT. WHAT HAPPENS AT CAMP STAYS AT CAMP!"

"We didn't even make it to camp! Waiting too long to poo or pee can be uncomfortable and can hurt you. Watch what happens when you put off using the restroom."

NO! DON'T TURN THE PAGE!

THE FIVE STAGES OF POO GRIEF

STAGE 1
If you're going on a long trip you may want to take a seat for a bit and see what happens but otherwise it can probably wait.

STAGE 2
The package has been delivered to your doorstep.

PACKAGE SHIPPED

PACKAGE EN ROUTE

PACKAGE DELIVERED

EMERGENCY

STAGE 3
It's urgent that you get to a toilet right away.

STAGE 4
Hurry up! If a toilet isn't available then your body can go in and out of stages 3 and 4 (aka poo contractions).

STAGE 5... TOO LATE.

Choose the correct restroom. Close and lock the door if it's a private bathroom. Choose the urinal or stall furthest away from others. No talking on the phone or in person. No eye contact.

TIP: If you know you're going to be noisy, turn on the tv or some music to flush out the sound. Put a towel under the crack of the door. Cough or flush the toilet during the noisy parts.

POOP QUIZ

1. Your phone rings while you're doing the doo. What do you do?

2. Identify 5 offenses in rule 5

_____
_____
_____
_____
_____

3. What are signs that you've been in the bathroom too long?
   A) A line is forming
   B) Bathroom light automatically turns off
   C) Legs fall asleep
   D) Any of the above

4. Which is the correct way to replace the TP role?

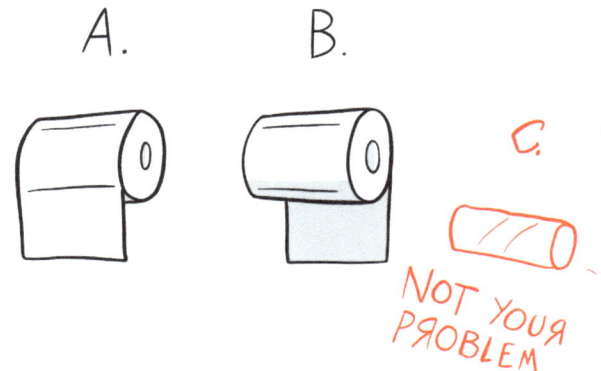

5. You've just entered the restroom. Which stall should you choose?

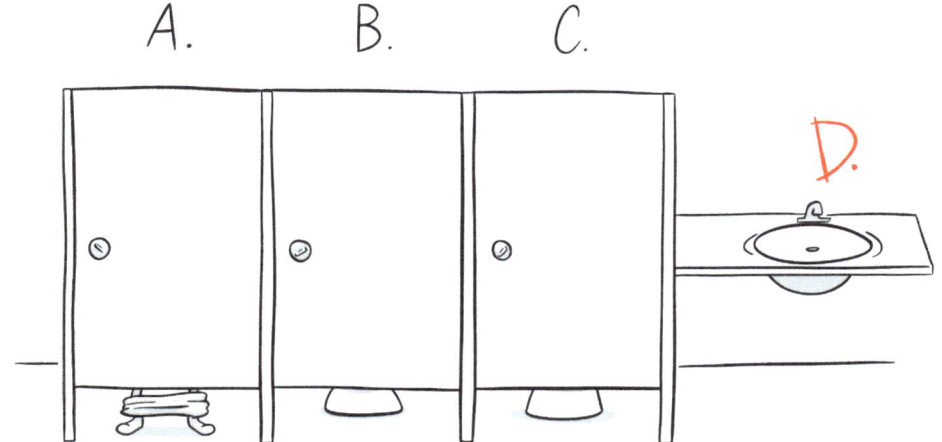

DELETED SCENES

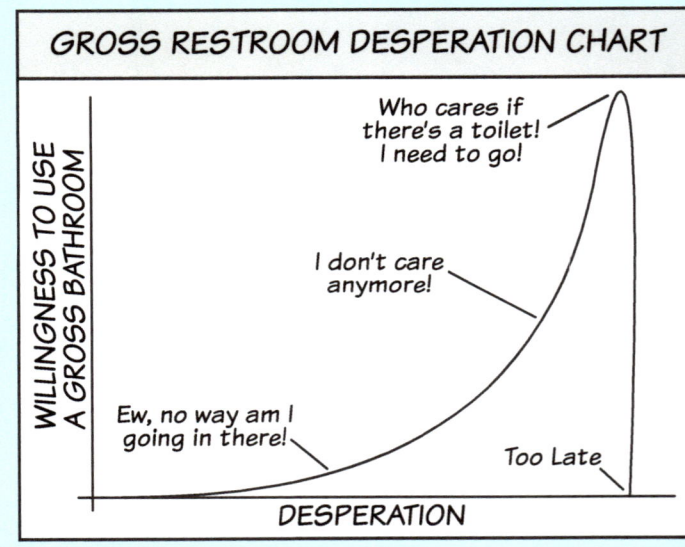

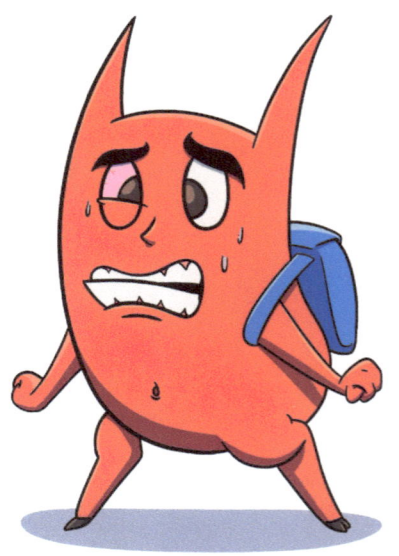

www.ingramcontent.com/pod-product-compliance
Lightning Source LLC
Chambersburg PA
CBHW042116040426
42449CB00002B/65